John Hickling

The Art of Speculation and Secrets of Wall Street fully explained

John Hickling

The Art of Speculation and Secrets of Wall Street fully explained

ISBN/EAN: 9783743318427

Manufactured in Europe, USA, Canada, Australia, Japa

Cover: Foto ©Suzi / pixelio.de

Manufactured and distributed by brebook publishing software
(www.brebook.com)

John Hickling

The Art of Speculation and Secrets of Wall Street fully explained

THE

ART OF SPECULATION

AND

SECRETS OF WALL STREET

FULLY EXPLAINED.

BY

.J. HICKLING & CO.,

Bankers and Stock Brokers,

72 BROADWAY AND 11 NEW STREET,

OPPOSITE STOCK AND
GOLD EXCHANGES,

CONTENTS.

PART FIRST.

Wall Street Finance.—The remarkable development of financial and commercial enterprise in the United States the last half century has astonished the whole civilized world, and Wall street during that time has become ·the great centre of finance and speculation.

The New York Stock Exchange is a new and spacious building devoted to the sale of Railroad Stocks, Bonds and other Securities. It extends from Broad street to New street, having an entrance on each side; also one in Wall street. The Custom House, Treasury, Private and National Banks, and other ·moneyed institutions, being in the immediate vicinity, form a perfect nucleus of wealth.

The Brokers' Little Game.—The hours in which the Bulls and Bears transact business are from 10 A. M. to 3 P. M, and any one wishing to view those animals in their daily pastimes can do so by entering the visitors' gallery. At the present time the Board of Brokers consist of upwards of one thousand members, and the aggregate amount of business which passes their hands in one year is computed at about fifteen thousand millions of dollars, or an average of nearly fifty millions a day. As fast as sales are made they are telegraphed all over the city, and thence to all parts of the country, so that a person thousands of miles away can take advantage of the fluctuations in the Stock Market, and have facilities for operating from day to day the same as a resident of New York City.

Cliques or Pools.—Men in Wall street, starting with a few hundred dollars, and observing the rules which guide leading speculators, have, by boldness and skillful manipulation, become the possessors of millions. These nabobs are continually formimg new enterprises, and frequently combine in controlling Railroad and other corporations. They tighten money; lock up gold, and raise or depress the price of stocks at will; indeed, their influence is felt in every financial community.

Very often a Bull Clique and a Bear Clique will form at the same time in opposition to each other—the one to raise prices, the other to lower them. The mystic working of these cliques produces an active market, when stocks change hands with great rapidity, often varying in price from 2 to 10 per cent. in one day, and 20 to 30 per cent. in a month.

Capital Required.—Until recent years it was considered indispensable to have a large capital in order to speculate, and thousands attracted to Wall street with a view to share the immense gains derived from dealing in stocks and other securities, have been deterred from operating, either from lack of capital or the requisite knowledge how to invest.

This is all changed. We are living in an age of progress, in which old systems and ideas must give place to new. By the aid of this pamphlet all may have an equal chance of reaping a golden harvest, and we shall show that men of small means may do a large business in stocks and bonds without incurring the usual risks, and yet succeed in a comparatively short time in making a fortune.

Privileges, or Puts and Calls.—It has

recently become quite popular to deal in stock Privileges, known as Puts, Calls and Double Privileges, not only with New York speculators, but more especially those living a distance away. We notice that many careful and shrewd operators adopt this plan, which seems likely to supersede all other methods of speculating on small capital.

Holders of these contracts are always protected from loss, and under any circumstances assume no risk or responsibility beyond the small amount paid for the Privilege; while if the market should favor them, their profits on $100 investments are as large as would, under the old system, require a capital of $5,000 to $20,000.

Stock Privileges, or Put and Call contracts, are of three kinds, viz:

A Put Privilege.

A Call Privilege.

A Double Privilege (or Straddle, which is a Put and a Call combined).

The first is used if you think stocks will decline.

The second is used if you think stocks will advance.

The third is used if you are uncertain which way they will go.

Each one of these Privileges is found of great advantage under certain circumstances; but Double Privileges are more frequently sought after, for, which ever way a stock may go beyond the price of the contract, a profit is certain.

How they Run.—These Privileges are issued by capitalists largely interested in certain stocks, and made generally for thirty days. The rates are about 2 per cent. away from the market price, but vary from time to time, and are higher or lower according to the feeling on the street or the activity of the market on the day of negotiation.

Each Privilege realizes a profit in proportion to the fluctuation beyond the price of the contract during the thirty days. A rise or fall of 1 per cent. gives a profit of $100 on a Call or Put for 100 shares of stock, 5 per cent. gives a profit of $500 on 100 shares of stock, and so on; but it must be remembered that the amount of profit will be regulated by the market price on the day the contract is closed. A Privilege may be closed any time during the thirty days—it is not necessary to wait until the day it expires.

The New System.—All the leading houses issue privileges on 100 shares of stock, but, to afford an equal opportunity to all who wish to make the experiment on a small scale at first, we have decided to issue Puts, Calls and Double Privileges on 50 shares, 25 shares, and. if desired, we are often in a position to issue them on 10 shares. We are at all times prepared to negotiate Privileges on Members of the Stock Exchange or responsible firms, and will issue our own contracts, or guarantee those

negotiated by us and pay the profits on same in
cash or by check immediately on presentation.

Commission on Puts and Calls.—Our

Commission on Puts and Calls is

$0.65 on 10 shares. ⎫
$1.50 on 25 shares. ⎪
$3.00 on 50 shares. ⎬ Single Put or Call.
$6.00 on 100 shares. ⎭

$1.25 on 10 shares. ⎫
$3.00 on 25 shares. ⎪
$6.00 on 50 shares. ⎬ Double Privileges.
$12.00 on 100 shares. ⎭

Price of 30 Day Privileges, including

commissions:

A Put or Call......on 10 shares costs. $10.65
A Put or Call......on 25 shares costs. 26.50
A Put or Call......on 50 shares costs. 53.00
A Put or Call......on 100 shares costs. 106.00
A Double Privilege on 10 shares costs. 21.25
A Double Privilege on 25 shares costs. 53.00
A Double Privilege on 50 shares costs. 106.00
A Double Privilege on 100 shares costs. 212.00

𝔓rofit on a 𝔓ut, $4,588.

To prove our assertion that money can be made easier in the New York Stock Market than anywhere else, we will first illustrate a Put Privilege.

On the 9th September, 1873, New York and Harlem Railroad Stock was selling at 140 after an advance of 26 per cent., or $2,600 on 100 shares. At that price it was quite reasonable to expect a decline, and supposing that to be your judgment, you obtain a Put on that stock, say at 137, costing $106 on 100 shares. The following would be a copy of the contract:

𝔉orm of 𝔓ut 𝔠ontract.

New York, Sept. 9th, 1873.

The bearer may Put or deliver to us one hundred shares of the capital stock of the New York and Harlem Railroad, at 137 per cent. par value, any time within 30 days from date. The undersigned is entitled to all dividends declared during that time.

Expires Oct. 9th, 1873.

J. HICKLING & CO.

Eleven days afterwards, Sept. 20th, N. Y. & Harlem fell to 90, and if you had closed the contract on that day you could have bought the stock in the market at 90 and Put or delivered it to us at 137, or we would pay you the cash difference of 47 per cent., and your profit would be as follows:

EXAMPLE.

Put on 100 N. Y. & H., Sept. 9th, at 137.......$13,700
Contract closed..........Sept. 20th, at 90....... ˙9,000

Profit to holder of Put... .... $4,700
Deduct amount paid for Privilege.............. 106

$4,594
Commission for closing contract................ 6

Net gain.. $4,588

The above profit is gained on an investment of $106. If you had taken a Put on 50 shares only, the profit would, of course, be half that sum, or $2,294, and a put on 25 shares, $1,147.

Profit on a Call, $9,388.—We will next show what you could do on a Call Privilege.

On the 11th November, 1872, Chicago and Northwestern Common was selling at 77 ; 12 days later, the 23d same month, it was 230. Supposing you decided to take a Call, say at 80, the following would be a copy of the contract we should send you:

Form of Call Contract.

New York, Nov. 11th, 1872.

The bearer may Call on us for one hundred shares of the common stock of the Chicago and Northwestern Railroad, at 80 per cent. par value, at any time within 30 days from date. The bearer is entitled to all dividends declared during that time.

Expires Dec. 11th, 1872.

J. HICKLING & Co.

A short time afterwards the stock advanced with a bound to 230, and we will suppose in your anxiety to realize you did not wait until it reached those figures, but Called the stock when it was 175. The difference between

80 — the price your Privilege enabled you
to buy it at from us — and 175 — at which
price you could have sold it in the market—
would be 95 per cent. or $9,500 profit on 100
shares. Instead of going through the form
of buying and selling the stock, we would
pay you the difference in cash.

Call on 100 N. W., closed Nov. 23d, at 175.......	$17,500
Price of contract issued Nov. 11th, at 80.......	8.000
	$9,500
Deduct cost of Privilege......................	106
	$9,394
Commission for closing contract...............	6
	$9,388

A Call on 50 shares of the same stock, costing $53, would have given a profit of $4,694;
on 25 shares, $2,347. This is taking the
stock at 175, but, as before stated, it rose to
230 — 55 per cent. higher — so that there was
an opportunity of realizing a much larger profit
than that given in the foregoing example.
You will, therefore, perceive we have rather
under-estimated the case than otherwise.

Double Privileges.—Your attention is now called to the last and most important Privilege—a Double Privilege or Straddle, which means both a Put and a Call in one contract. The great advantage of a Straddle is, that a person entirely unacquainted with stocks, and living thousands of miles from New York, can operate with more certainty—having two chances to gain and only one to lose. If the stock should rise, the holder of a Double Privilege makes a profit on the Call side ; if it should decline, he gains on the Put side. It is a matter of indifference which way it goes, for he makes a profit in either case. The only chance of losing is where the stock remains almost stationary, which is a very rare occurrence indeed. Many New York speculators adopt this method, which enables them to operate largely with the chances of securing a fortune on a single transaction, while the risk is merely nominal. We recommend all to buy a Double Privilege in preference to a Put or Call. It often happens, as in the case of Northwestern, that a stock may be high and yet advance from 10 to 100 per cent. in thirty days, to the surprise of every one but those in the Pool. The fiercest battle may be waging between the Bulls and Bears, without any apparent victory on either side, but the holder of a Double Privilege may look on the wreck of millions and calmly watch the result without fear of the consequences, and secure his profit at the most favorable opportunity. We make these suggestions to show that it is wise to take a Double Privilege in preference to a simple Put or Call.

Profit $16,880.—We will now illustrate what can be done with a Double Privilege. Western Union Telegraph fluctuated in less than one month 38 per cent. It was selling at 92 on the 3d September, 1873, and everything looked bright and prosperous. The company had made the most favorable reports, and at that time were erecting a magnificent new building on Broadway, to meet the requirements of their increased business. Holders of the stock were confident that the flourishing condition of W. U. Tel. would attract new purchasers and thereby enhance its value. But alas! the panic came, and their hopes vanished away "like the baseless fabric of a vision," and in less than three weeks Western Union was 54.

Now, suppose you had taken a Straddle on 500 shares of that stock at 90 and 94—2 per cent. from the market each way, the contract would read as follows:

Form of Double Privilege.

New York, Sept. 3, 1873.

The bearer may *Put or deliver to us Five Hundred Shares of the Capital Stock of the Western Union Telegraph Co. at 90 per cent., par value, any time within thirty days from date.*

Or the bearer may call on us for Five Hundred Shares of the above named Stock at 94 per cent., par value, any time during the thirty days.

All dividends declared during that time, in either case, go with the stock.

Expires Oct. 3d.

J. HICKLING & CO.

Seventeen days later, when the stock was selling at 54, you could have closed the Privilege on the Put side, and we would either buy the 500 shares at 90, or pay you the difference between 90 and 54, the then market price, giving you a profit of $16,880.

EXAMPLE.

Double Privilege on 500 W. U. Tel., Sept. 3, at 90..	$45,000
Put closed Sept. 20th at 54..................	27,000
	$18,000
Cost of Privilege........................	1,060
	$16,940
Commission for closing contract...............	60
	$16,880

Double Privileges give the holders all the benefits of the fluctuations of the market, and are, in our opinion, the most profitable investments that can be made. Old and experienced speculators invariably prefer this plan of operating on small capital. The new beginner is very apt to be a Bull, but experience shows that, under the most apparently favorable circumstances for a rise, stocks will often decline. Therefore, those who obtain Double Privileges are sure to be on the right side. They frequently give a profit, both on a rise and fall of the stock. For instance, if you held a Double Privilege on 100 shares of Erie, at 50—2 per cent. from the market each way, and the stock rose to 60, there would be a profit of $800 on the Call side, and if, before the 30 days expired, it fell to 40, you would make $800 more on the Put.

Sixteen Chances to One.—By the new system adopted by us you are enabled to take any number of shares your means or inclination may prompt. You could take a Double Privilege on 10 shares of stock for $21.25, including our commission. If you wished to invest in 100 shares, costing $212, you might select four different stocks, 25 shares each, so that if one failed to give a profit, the remaining three would surely make up for the loss. Or you could have a Double Privilege on eight different stocks, 25 shares each, costing $424. In the latter case it would be equal to eight Calls and eight Puts on eight different stocks, or sixteen chances to win against one to lose.

Facts and Figures.—All the foregoing quotations occurred on the dates mentioned, and are taken from the recorded prices at the Stock Exchange. We could refer to many other instances of similar fluctuations, but that is unnecessary; one illustration will serve our purpose as well as a thousand. We wish to state, however, that what has once occurred in stocks may, and no. doubt will, occur again; and, therefore, the same opportunities of making money in the past will present themselves in the future. Of course we do not wish to lead any one to suppose that such large profits can be expected on every transaction; but we may, with almost a certainty, reckon on a profit of 50 to 500 per cent. on the amount invested. That large fortunes are frequently made is a fact. Men whose names are as familiar as household words, and indeed nearly all the leading speculators of the present day have found their first stepping stone to wealth in Wall street.

The Lion's Share.—The question will naturally arise "How is it that capitalists will issue these privileges and take the risk of paying these large profits?" The answer is very simple, and, when explained, will be readily understood. It does not follow that because the maker of a Privilege pays a large profit that he sustains the loss. In the majority of cases he actually gains by the transaction.

Suppose a large operator buys 1,000 shares of Panama at 95 for a rise, and sells a Call on the same stock at 100, for which he receives 1 per cent. or $1,000 on 1,000 shares. Panama advances to 130, and the holder of Call closes the contract with a profit of 30 per cent. or $30,000. The maker of Privilege being called upon to pay this profit, he sells out his stock at the advanced price, which leaves him, after satisfying the claim, a clear gain of $6,000.

In the case of the Put, another speculator " sells short "* 1,000 shares of Panama at 95 for a decline, which he desires to buy at a reduced price. He then sells a Put, say at 90, and before the thirty days expire, if the stock falls to 60 and the holder of the Put closes the contract, he is glad to buy the stock, which enables him to pay the profit and have $6,000 left, as in the preceding case, only the operation is reversed. It will thus be seen that both parties make a profit—the holder of the Privilege, however, receiving the lion's share.

This also explains how we are protected in issuing Double Privileges. It is difficult to obtain both a Put and a Call from the same party, but we can always negotiate a Put from one and a Call from another, which protects us on both sides, for, if the stock should decline, we Put it to the maker of the contract, and, if it should advance, we Call it in the same manner, paying the profit in either case to our customer, less commission.

INSTRUCTIONS

FOR

ORDERING PRIVILEGES.

☞ All orders sent by mail must be accompanied by the cash. either in registered letter, by Postal Money Order, Bank Draft or Express.

☞ Urgent orders may be sent by telegraph, in which case the money should be deposited at the branch office of the Western Union Telegraph Company where you reside, when the amount will be transferred to us by the Company in New York, and a telegraphic answer returned immediately the order is executed.

☞ Privileges may be ordered by express, and the money paid on delivery—C. O. D.

☞ When orders are prepaid Privileges will be sent by return mail same day as received, or delivered to authorized agents.

☞   If requested, we will make investments as low as $10.65, $21.25, $26.50, $53, or $106 in Privileges, selecting such stocks as we believe will be most active. Our experience often enables us to give valuable suggestions, and we take pleasure in furnishing our customers with all information in our power tending to promote their interests.

☞   Those who are undecided which way the market will go should always order a Put and a Call on the same stock, for, whichever way it varies, they are certain to make a profit. This is called a Double Privilege, and costs $21.25 for 10 shares, $53 for 25 shares, $106 for 50 shares, and $212 for 100 shares.

☞   For the benefit of those living a great distance from New York we will, when requested, hold Privileges, and endeavor to close them at the most favorable opportunity. Those wishing contracts closed in this manner should state their views as regards profits, to a certain extent, to guide us as far as possible in carrying out their instructions with satisfaction to all concerned.

☞ When the profit on a Privilege is paid the contract must be surrendered to us and returned in every instance, without fail, to enable us to collect counter claims.

☞ In corresponding, be careful to inform us how your letters should be addressed, giving name, residence, town, county and State as plainly as possible, to facilitate quick despatch. Delay is sometimes occasioned by failure to follow this rule, and that is our apology for making these remarks. Letters requiring answers at all times receive our prompt attention. All we ask is your coöperation.

☞ All correspondence strictly private and confidential.

Address all orders and communications,

J. HICKLING & CO.,

72 BROADWAY,

New York.

PART SECOND.

BUYING AND SELLING STOCKS ON MARGIN.
INVESTMENTS IN STOCKS, BONDS, Etc.

Terms Used in Wall Street.—In the first
part of this book we have recommended the
Put and Call system as eminently adapted for
operating in stocks on a limited capital, and
it will be remembered that persons who wish
to start on a small scale at first, can, by order-
ing through us, make the experiment on as
small sums as $10.65, $21.25, $26.50, $53 and
$106. We will now consider buying and selling
stocks on margin, or as an investment, and
point out the various terms used by the
brokers, so that those unacquainted with stock
operations may be familiar with their meaning
and significance.

Speculation.—And, first of all, what is speculation? It is buying something you do not
need for present use, with the expectation of
selling it at some future time at a profit. The
love of gain is an inherent principle of human
nature, and, in one sense, the foundation of all
enterprise. The desire to make money is the
mainspring of speculation. The merchant who
buys a larger quantity of merchandise than is
necessary to supply his present demands *specu-*
lates, either because he considers certain goods
cheap or is anxious to secure a monopoly in
them for his own exclusive benefit. The miller,
anticipating a bad harvest, buys up all the grain
his means and credit will permit, and waits his
opportunity of selling it when there is a
scarcity in the market and he can command
his own price. He may, by economy, per-
severance and years of close application to
business, succeed in making a competency as
the fruits of honest industry; but he prefers to
adopt a quicker method, and enters the arena of
speculation, which opens to him the way of

making as much money in a single year as would, by the slow, plodding process, consume nearly a whole lifetime.

The successful speculator will always look ahead and watch the signs of the times. Scanning the distant horizon in the commercial and financial world, he will foresee "Coming events which cast their shadows before," and be the first in the field to profit by them. In a general way the result of speculation will depend upon the exercise of good judgment, but in some instances will be governed by circumstances over which we have no control. However, the fact remains, if we understand it aright, that the wealthiest men in all branches of business are speculators. The old maxim of " buying cheap and selling dear " is the *sine qua non* of speculation, and the same principle which rules trade and commerce equally applies to stocks. A wealthy speculator in Wall street being asked one day how he made his money, replied, "I bought with the rise." Another retired gentleman, in answer to the same question, replied, " I sold with the fall." Each was equally successful, though taking a different course.

Margin.—A margin is a sum of money deposited with a broker as security for buying stock when the speculator has not sufficient capital to pay for it or does not wish to invest his own money. The amount of margin required is generally about 10 per cent. of the par value of the stock ($10,000), which would be $1,000 on every 100 shares.

Carrying Stock.—Supposing you want 100 shares of New York Central and Hudson at 90, you give your broker the order and $1,000 as margin. He then buys the stock which, at $90 a share, would cost $9,000, and furnishes the balance of $8,000 to complete the purchase, charging you interest on that amount until the stock is sold.

Commission.—The commission for buying or selling stock is ⅛ per cent., or $12.50 on 100 shares, and is uniformly the same, irrespective of the value of the stock. For instance, a hundred shares of Union Pacific at 30 would cost $3,000, while 100 New York and Harlem at 130, would cost $13,000. Yet the commission in each case would be the same.

Options.—Stock sold for cash is delivered on the same day, but if sold regular it is delivered on the following day. Under certain conditions of the market the difference between cash and regular is sometimes as much as 1 and 2 per cent. The seller may ask for three days' grace before delivering the stock, which is called seller's option (s. 3), or the buyer may ask for 10 days (b. 10), and that would be a condition of the transaction.

The Brokers' Rule.—Whatever the terms of the sale may be, they must be scrupulously observed by both parties, and the contract carried out in perfect good faith. Should any dispute arise, however, the case is referred to a committee of the Board, who decide the question on its merits, according to the laws and regulations which are made for the mutual protection of all members of the Association, and their decision is final. If any member should refuse to conform to that decision, or fail in any manner to fulfil his engagements, he is either fined or suspended from the Board, as the penalty may require.

𝕷ong of 𝕾tocks, or a 𝕭ull.—The broker

now having the 100 shares of New York Central in his possession, which he is carrying for you on margin, makes you Long of Stock. A rise of 1 per cent. in the market is equal to $1 a share, $100 on 100 shares, $1,000 on 1,000 shares, and so on

𝕾elling 𝕺ut.—We will suppose New York

Central rose to 105, at which price you decide to sell the 100 shares bought at 90. The profit would be 15 per cent. or $1,500.

EXAMPLE.

Sold　100 shares N. Y. Cen. at 105...........$10,500
Bought 100 shares N. Y. Cen. at 90........... 9,000
$1,500

The transaction being closed, the $1,500 is added to tho $1,000 deposited in the first instance, and placed to your credit, subject to your order, and bearing interest at the rate of 7 per cent. per annum until again invested.

Call Loans.—When a broker is carrying more stock for his customers than his capital will pay for, he borrows money from another broker, giving a portion of stock in his possession as collateral security. This is a Call Loan, or Borrowing on Demand.

Tight Money Market.—The usual rates for Call Loans are 7 per cent., but when money is tight higher rates prevail. This is done by withdrawing greenbacks from circulation, which compels those who want money to pay whatever is asked for it—sometimes as high as 1, 2 and 3 per cent. a day. In the commercial world every monopoly exerts its influence on the community, and it is the same in financial affairs. The combined action of a clique in making money scarce answers a double purpose. The object of locking up greenbacks is not so much to force borrowers to pay an extortionate rate for its use, as to compel those who are long of stocks to sell out. The chief aim is to make it so expensive to carry stocks that holders will unload. In proportion as the screws are tightened the number of operators offering stocks on the market increase, until, in the hurry and confusion, a temporary panic ensues, and prices fall 5 or 10 per cent. The clique then step in and buy, and when sufficiently loaded, the money locked up is again put into circulation and loaned at low rates, the effect of which is to send prices up. As before, stocks declined with a stringent money market, so, when money becomes easy, they advance, enabling the clique to sell out at a handsome profit.

Short of Stocks, or a Bear.

—A short sale is a contract to sell and deliver a stock which you do not own. You sell what you have not got, in the expectation of buying it back at a lower price. Being short of stock is like being short of money that you are obliged to pay, so you have to borrow, trusting to the future to make good the loan. As a person Long of Stocks buys for a rise, so one Short of Stocks sells for a decline. Having sold short, and borrowed the stock for delivery, you must ,pay it back ; that is, you must buy it back at some time before the transaction can be closed. If you buy it back cheaper, you gain ; if you pay more for it, you lose.

Covering a Short Sale.—We will suppose you sell short 200 Lake Shore at 80. As you have not got the stock, you borrow it for delivery to the purchaser, who gives you a certified check for $16,000 in payment. You then pass this check over to the party who loaned you the stock, as security, and if Lake Shore in the meantime declines to 75 you buy 200 shares in the market, costing $15,000, and return the borrowed stock, receiving back the $16,000 and making a profit of $1,000. Should Lake Shore go up to 85 and you were called

upon for the stock, you would be compelled to buy it in the market, costing $17,000, which would entail a loss of $1,000.

If you did not take the latter course, when the stock advanced you would have to deposit $1,000 more as security to the loaner, as it would be worth that much more in the market. By thus protecting your short sale a loss would not necessarily follow, for you could stay short and wait for a sufficient decline to make a profit.

Corners.—A corner in stocks is another manipulation of the cliques, but of very rare occurrence, as it is a difficult thing to accomplish. To be "forewarned is to be forearmed," and as it is possible to have a corner in stocks at any time, the speculator should endeavor at all times to be prepared for such a contingency. There is always a clique buying up all they can of a certain stock, and very often the Bears are selling it at the same time. If the Bulls succeed in getting the control when there is a large short interest in the market, they will immediately raise the price and vigorously continue to do so until the shorts have covered, which, of course, they cannot do without loss. The clique holding all the available stock, the Bears, or shorts, cannot borrow any from other brokers, and are cornered. They are, therefore, compelled to buy from the clique at whatever price they choose to ask. When this occurs those who cover first sustain the least loss, but those who hold on to the last will suffer the most.

Modus Operandi.—There are certain principles underlying the successful application of stock speculations which, if understood, will guide the operator in taking advantage of the market. It must always be remembered that two forces are continually at work in Wall street, the effects of which you must endeavor to turn to your own profit. The great secret of success is, never let your neighbor know what you are doing. Let this be your motto, and never lose sight of its importance—for to secrecy, more than anything else, all the leading men on the street to-day owe their position and wealth.

Never speculate beyond your means; there are many influences at work to tempt the operator to rush blindly into the stream of speculation and go beyond his depth. The speculator who is not guided by the exercise of discretion and common sense should not complain if his indiscriminate investments terminate in disaster. Rumors and false reports are commonly resorted to for the purpose of producing certain effects. The very circumstance calculated in your mind to produce a rise, may have been announced for a contrary purpose. The news which you regard as fresh may have been known and acted upon hours previous to your entering the market, and a sudden break down follow an upward movement, so that, while congratulating yourself on a sure thing, you may be actually left out in the cold. In such instances it is often best to act on your own judgment, using caution or boldness as necessity may require.

The price of stocks is often influenced by money, which like all other commodities is governed by the law of supply and demand.

When an abundance of money is in circulation it is more easily obtained at low rates, so you buy stocks because it is easy to carry them. On the other hand, if money is scarce, the rates become higher, you therefore sell to avoid the expense of carrying.

It is not necessary to be present in Wall street in order to operate in stocks. There is a large class who never or seldom visit even their brokers' offices, sending their orders by letter or telegram. Persons away from New York can give instructions to their brokers, who will carry out all orders the same as though their customers were present in person.

Double Operations.—After selling out your stock when the price has advanced considerably, and you believe there will be a reaction, you may determine to sell short—that is, you sell double the number of shares which you were carrying. For instance, if you were long of 500 shares of Toledo and Wabash at 40, and the price went up to 55, you would sell the 500 shares at 15 per cent. profit, or $7,500, but if you believed, after such an advance, that Wabash would decline in price, you would sell short 500 extra, and if it afterwards fell to 45 you could cover at a profit of 10 per cent. or $5,000, closing the transaction with a profit both ways, making altogether $12,500 by the double operation.

Profit, $13,700.—Let us take for example Western Union Telegraph, one of the most active stocks, and see what could have been done in the latter part of 1873—from Sept. 15th to Dec. 6th. During that time the recorded price will show eight large fluctuations, which, if the speculator had secured the advantage of by double operations on 100 shares of stock would have yielded a small fortune on an investment of $1,000 in less than three months.

EXAMPLE.

1873.									
Sept. 15.	Sold Short.	100 W. U.,	at 90..		....	$9,000
Oct. 2.	Bought	200 " "	" 60.	$12,000		
Oct. 5.	Sold	200 " "	" 73	....	14,600
Oct. 15.	Bought	200 " "	" 45..	9,000		
Oct. 23.	Sold ...:....	200 " "	" 59	....	11,800
Nov. 1.	Bought	200 " "	" 43..	8,600		
Nov. 17.	Sold	200 " "	" 60..	....	12,000
Nov. 19.	Bought	200 " "	" 57..	11,400		
Dec. 6.	Sold	100 " "	" 73	....	7,300

$41,000 $54,700
                          41,000

Profit $13,700

Investments.—"How shall I invest my money?" is ever and anon the cry of the merchant, tradesman, clergyman or mechanic. All kinds of experiments are made and many methods employed to secure the desired result. Every decade brings forth some new mania which takes hold of the public. At one time there will be a rush for real estate, and every man thinks it his first duty to buy a home for his family. The motive is a worthy one, but where a man pays only a small amount down, depending upon his future resources to complete the purchase, he generally fails in realizing his expectations; for, should he be unable to meet an installment or interest on a mortgage, a foreclosure takes place, and he is not only deprived of the property, but loses the whole amount paid. Others think they have found the philosopher's stone in putting money on bond and mortgage, believing they are secured against all contingencies, but it is a well known fact that thousands have been ruined by this form of investment. The last five years have been marked by a fictitious value in nearly every description of property, and the reaction which has since taken place shows a depreciation of 40 per cent., and even more. We contend and are convinced that investments in stocks, bonds, or other convertible securities, are much more profitable and attended with much less risk.

There is, of course, some degree of risk in every form of investment. The tradesman who opens a store can have no guarantee beforehand that his business will prove a success. He may commence with a capital of $5,000 or $50,000, but it is after all a speculation, which, it is needless to say, often ends in failure. Let us for a moment glance at what is accomplished by the merchant or tradesman. Statistics show the startling fact that over ninety out of a hundred men fail in business, either becoming bankrupt or insolvent at some period of their career. There are certainly many brilliant examples of remarkable prosperity to be found in commercial circles, but they are the exceptions which prove the rule.

The merchant, to be successful, must employ the proper means of success, and have considerable capital. He must subject himself to the greatest diligence, and exercise the strictest economy in conducting his affairs. He must be an expert buyer, and have a perfect knowledge of values. Then he is dependent upon the system of credit, and, although using great care and discrimination in selecting his customers, he cannot avoid contracting bad debts.

Following up the merchant, after years of persevering industry and many changes of fortune, we find his stock increased, his liabilities increased, and a large increase of bad debts to the account of profit and loss. A commercial crisis ensues. The market is glutted, but no buyers. Creditors' bills become due, but cannot be met. As a *dernier resort* the merchant tries *inflation*, thereby increasing his obligations by renewed promises to pay on paper. This is "the last straw that breaks the camel's back." Stretching every nerve in the vain endeavor to maintain his honor and credit, he finally

becomes a victim to misfortune. His dimin-
ished assets, consisting of a depreciated stock
and a list of uncollectable accounts, are handed
over to his creditors, who close the scene by
taking full possession of his affairs.

Investments in stocks and bonds, while offering equal, and, in many instances, superior pros-
pects for making money, present advantages
not to be found in any other pursuit. The
investor in Wall street can select such securities as will pay dividends at double the rates
of interest allowed by the banks, and have full
personal control of the same. His capital is
not locked up, as in the case of the merchant
who gives long credit. His securities have
always a marketable cash value, convertible
into greenbacks at an hour's notice, enabling
him to sell out his interest whenever he
thinks well. Should he wish to visit Europe on
business or pleasure, he can leave his securities locked up until his return. If he wishes
to remain at home, instead of his time being
engrossed in the monotonous routine of a store
or counting room, he has leisure to enter into

the intellectual pleasures or physical recreations of life, without detriment to his pecuniary interests. In fine, he has increased facilities for watching affairs of national importance, and the development of the resources of the country opens to him a new and wide field for the study of finance.

STATE BONDS.

ARKANSAS ....6s, F. D; 7s, R. R.; 7s, Levee.
CALIFORNIA..................7s, 1877–'91.
CONNECTICUT...............6s, 1831–'84; Exempt 1855.
GEORGIA................6ª, various; 7s, 1866.
ILLINOIS......................6s, 1878–'80.
KENTUCKY......,............6s.
LOUISIANA..................6s, various; 8s, 1886.
MARYLAND ....6s, 1890; various.
MASSACHUSETTS...........5s; 6s, guar'd.
MICHIGAN...................6s, 1873–'83; 7s, 1890.
MAINE......................6s, various.
MISSOURI.... ....6s, various.
 NEW HAMPSHIRE ....6s, various.
 NEW JERSEY................6s, various.
NEW YORK...................5s, 1875; 6s, C. L.; 7s, B. L.
NORTH CAROLINA...........6s, old; N. C.: F. A.; Sp. Tax.
OHIO..........................6s, 1875–'86.
PENNSYLVANIA..............5s, 6s of 1867—1st, 2d and 3d.
RHODE ISLAND..............6s, various.
SOUTH CAROLINA.,.........6s, old and new.
TENNESSEE.................6s, old; ex. coupon.
VIRGINIA...................6s, old and new; Cons.; Def'd.

	1860	1861	1862	1863	1864	1865	1866	1867	1868	1869	1870	1871	1872	1873
Canton Im. Co.	23/14	15/8	18/10	44/17	71/26	47/26	62/42	53/41	64/45	68/48	73/55	186/68	107/76	110/66
Chicago & Northwestern	84/42	62/30	…	50/16	88/34	40/20	62/24	65/30	97/68	94/63	85/69	92/51	230/66	85/31
Chicago & Rock Island	99/86	102/90	85/60	123/82	149/86	113/81	123/80	105/85	118/85	138/101	126/101	130/94	118/101	117/63
Clev., Col., Cin. & Ind.	…	…	145/103	181/147	182/146	180/124	123/110	111/97	110/74	82/62	83/73	94/81	95/88	94/65
Col., Chic. & Ind. Cen.	…	…	…	…	…	…	…	…	…	59/19	22/15	24/15	42/19	43/16
Del., Lack. & Western	99/54	84/65	130/80	198/130	265/195	225/176	162/124	130/109	132/107	120/104	112/100	111/102	112/91	106/79
Erie	…	…	65/31	122/66	126/82	98/44	97/65	77/52	81/36	42/21	28/20	35/18	75/30	69/36
Harlem	24/8	17/8	26/11	179/27	285/86	77/75	99/85	118/93	131/112	168/125	150/130	135/117	130/108	139/90
Illinois Central	89/51	88/55	84/65	138/81	138/110	138/90	131/112	135/111	159/133	147/130	145/131	139/132	140/119	126/90
Lake Shore & M. S.	…	…	…	…	…	…	101/66	86/64	94/80	109/83	102/84	116/85	98/83	97/57

	1873	1872	1871	1870	1869	1868	1867	1866	1865	1864	1863	1862	1861	1860
Michigan Central	110/65	120/113	120/114	126/116	136/114	129/106	114/102	117/105						
Milwaukee & St. Paul	62/21	64/51	64/48	75/52	81/61	111/46	64/28	64/41						
New Jersey Central	106/86	113/98	114/100	110/92	122/86	126/110	125/118	132/104						
New York Cent. & H.	106/77	101/89	101/90	102/86	217/164	154/110	118/96	123/86						
Ohio & Miss.	49/31	51/40	54/	42/27	39/22	34/28	29/20		34/19	69/32				
Panama	130/77	148/72	76/49	170/70	348/193	369/290	312/264	279/236	279/203	300/200	290/171	170/110	121/97	116/66
Pacific Mail S. S. Co.	76/25	95/63	58/39	46/30	123/42	130/86	178/108	246/160	329/151	325/219	248/136	137/91	100/60	107/74
Quicksilver	46/18	49/26	27/5	15/4	26/12	32/19	45/15	68/36	101/40	101/45	72/14			
Toledo, Wabash & W.	75/32	50/64	68/48	61/43	88/49	67/42	62/34	66/31	61/39	75/52	39/36			
West. Union Tel. Co.	94/43	88/67	71/44	46/31	44/32	38/33	50/3	70/43						

RAILROAD STATISTICS.

		Capital Stock.	No. of Miles.
Canton Land Company		$731,250	....
Cleveland and Pittsburg		11,236,150	225
Columbus, Chicago & Ind. Central		11,328,568	587
Chicago and Northwestern	Common.	15,000,000	1,459
" " "	Preferred	1,000,000	....
Chicago, Rock Island and Pacific		24,999,500	957
Delaware, Lackawanna & Western		23,500,000	618
Erie Railway	Common.	78,000,000	1,032
"	Preferred	8,536,910	....
Hannibal and Saint Joseph	Common.	9,167,700	275
" "	Preferred	5,087,224	....
Lake Shore and Michigan Southern		50,000,000	1,136
Milwaukee and Saint Paul	Common.	15,398,561	1,395
" "	Preferred	12,274,483	...
New Jersey Central		20,000,000	291
New York Central and Hudson		89,428,330	1,032
New York and Harlem		9,000,000	132
Ohio and Mississippi	Common.	20,000,000	393
" "	Preferred	4,030,000	....
Pacific Mail Steamship Co.		20,000,000	....
Panama Railroad		7,000,000	47
Quicksilver Mining Co.	Common.	4,291,300	....
" "	Preferred	5,708,700	....
Toledo, Wabash and Western	Common.	15,000,000	905
" "	Preferred	1,000,000	....
Union Pacific R. R.		36,745,000	1,039
Western Union Telegraph Co.		41,073,410	....

The above shows the amount of capital and number of miles of some of the principal Railroads.

Where there is Common and Preferred Stock of the same line, the latter takes precedence. Should a dividend be declared, the Preferred Stock would receive the first benefit.

LIST OF STOCKS

DEALT IN AT THE

NEW YORK STOCK EXCHANGE.

Ad. Ex.	Adams Express.
Am. Ex.	American Express.
A. Dist. T.	American District Telegraph Co.
A. & P., P'd.	Atlantic and Pacific Tel. Co., Preferred.
A. & T. H.	Alton and Terre Haute.
A. & T. H., P'd.	Alton and Terre Haute, Preferred.
B. H. & E.	Boston, Hartford and Erie.
N. W.	Chicago and Northwestern.
N. W., P'd.	Chicago and Northwestern, Preferred.
R. I.	Chicago, Rock Island and Pacific.
C., Bur. & Q.	Chicago, Burlington and Quincy.
C. & A.	Chicago and Alton.
C., C. & I. C.	Columbus, Chicago and Indiana Central.
C., C., C. & I.	Cleveland, Columbus, Cin. and Indiana.
Clev. & P.	Cleveland and Pittsburg.
Con. Coal.	Consolidation Coal Co.
Cen. P.	Central Pacific.
Can.	Canton Improvement Co.
D., L. & W.	Delaware, Lackawanna and Western.
E.	Erie Railway.
E., P'd.	Erie Railway, Preferred.
H. & St. Jo.	Hannibal and St. Joseph.
H. & St. Jo., P'd.	Hannibal and St. Joseph, Preferred.
Ill. Cen.	Illinois Central.
L. S.	Lake Shore and Michigan Southern.
M. C.	Michigan Central.
Mo. Pac.	Missouri Pacific.
K. & T.	Missouri, Kansas and Texas.
M. L. & M.	Mariposa Land and Mining Co.
M. & E.	Morris and Essex.
Mil. & St. P.	Milwaukee and St. Paul.
Mil. & St. P., P'd.	Milwaukee and St. Paul, Preferred.
N. Y. Cen.	New York Central and Hudson River.
N. Y. & N. H.	New York, New Haven and Hartford.
Har.	New York and Harlem.
N. J. Cen.	New Jersey Central.
N. J. So.	New Jersey Southern.
O. & M.	Ohio and Mississippi.
O. & M., P'd.	Ohio and Mississippi, Preferred.
P. M.	Pacific Mail Steamship Co.
Pan.	Panama Railroad.
P. & Ft. W.	Pittsburg and Fort Wayne.
Qu. M.	Quicksilver Mining Co.
Qu. M., P'd.	Quicksilver Mining Co., Preferred.
Iron M.	Saint Louis and Iron Mountain.
Sp. M. Coal.	Spring Mountain Coal Co.
Wab.	Toledo, Wabash and Western.
U. S.	United States Express.
U. P.	Union Pacific.
W. F.	Wells, Fargo & Co. Express.
W. U.	Western Union Telegraph Co.

NOTES.

Money may be sent by Postal Money Order or in Registered Letter; large amounts by Express or Bank Draft made payable in New York to our order.

Gold, Stocks or Bonds may be sent safely by Express, securely sealed, and the amount marked on outside of package.

Urgent orders may be sent by Telegraph, and the money deposited at the nearest branch office of the Western Union Telegraph Company, when the amount will be transferred to us by the company in New York, and telegraphic answer returned immediately the order is executed.

In corresponding, please be careful to inform us how letters should be addressed, giving Name, Residence or Box, Town, County and State, as plainly as possible, to ensure quick returns. Delay is sometimes occasioned by failure to observe this rule, and that is our apology for making these remarks.

Letters of inquiry will receive our prompt attention.

Address all orders and communications,

J. HICKLING & CO.,

72 Broadway,

New York.

THE

ART OF SPECULATION

AND

SECRETS OF WALL STREET

FULLY EXPLAINED.

— • • —

BY

J. HICKLING & CO.,

Bankers and Stock Brokers,

72 BROADWAY AND 11 NEW STREET,

GOLD EXCHANGES, } NEW YORK.